Hidden Meanings

A Comedy

Michael Snelgrove

A SAMUEL FRENCH ACTING EDITION

SAMUEL FRENCH

FOUNDED 1830

SAMUELFRENCH.COM
SAMUELFRENCH-LONDON.CO.UK

FOR PRODUCTION ENQUIRIES

UNITED STATES AND CANADA
Info@SamuelFrench.com
1-866-598-8449
UNITED KINGDOM AND EUROPE
Plays@SamuelFrench-London.co.uk
020-7255-4302

Each title is subject to availability from Samuel French, depending upon country of performance. Please be aware that *HIDDEN MEANINGS* may not be licensed by Samuel French in your territory. Professional and amateur producers should contact the nearest Samuel French office or licensing partner to verify availability.

Please refer to page 30 for further copyright information.

CHARACTERS

Professor Moriarty/Charles Meaning
Holmes/Rodney Carson
Dr Watson/George Humby
Mrs Hudson/Edna
Sylvia Carson
Inspector Jobling
Moira Meaning
Glenda
Deirdre, Edna's daughter

Chorus of policemen (optional)

This play is dedicated to Martin Kempton and John Crowhurst and all their partners in crime

HIDDEN MEANINGS

The play is set in the Carsons' sitting-room which bears a remarkable resemblance to Sherlock Holmes's room at 221b Baker Street. There is a door upstage L and a large walk-in cupboard upstage R. Upstage C are a pair of curtains seemingly covering a window and behind these is a rostrum and a projection screen (see ground plan). Next to the cupboard is a drinks table and downstage L is a dresser covered with books and a chemistry set. The room's general appearance is cluttered and untidy with various bric-à-brac, Victoriana, mementoes and books

In the darkness there is the sound of rushing water and "The Ride of the Valkyries" playing very loudly. The curtains upstage C open to reveal an epic struggle being played out in silhouette on the rostrum; the life and death fight between Sherlock Holmes and Professor Moriarty at the Reichenbach Falls. As they wrestle the advantage shifts constantly and as it reaches a climax both men seem on the brink of toppling into the abyss

"Moriarty" Damn you, Sherlock Holmes! Damn you!
"Holmes" Save your breath, Professor Moriarty! The world shall be rid of your evil for ever!

Holmes disengages himself, steps back and draws a pistol

"Moriarty" No! No!

He tries to grab the pistol but "Holmes" fires. "Moriarty" clutches his stomach, groans and then falls with a scream long enough to suggest a very long drop into the Falls. "Holmes" stands looking down and then starts to laugh as the curtains upstage C close slowly and the Lights fade to a Black-out. At the same time "The Ride of the Valkyries" and the sound of rushing water fade

There is a short pause and then a violin is heard playing, plangent, beautiful, and eerie. After a few seconds the rapturous tone begins to falter and mistakes and wrong notes creep in until all that is left is a horrible cacophany

A spot comes up downstage C *to reveal Sherlock Holmes, or somebody very like him, striking a pose with a violin under his chin, his eyes narrowed looking out into the audience*

"Holmes" For the detective, Watson, the fundamental problem is one of *observation* and the precise application of *logic*. From a man's hands, from the cut of his trousers, from his fingernails and from the knees of his trousers we may observe and deduce all that is essential about his character. And his trousers. There is no problem so great, no crime so monstrous, that it cannot be solved by a keen eye and a clear brain. Logic, I would presume to add, *is* order, and the detective—the truly great detective—is one of Nature's most accomplished ordering machines. Do you not consider that to be so, Watson?

There is no response

Watson?

The Lights come up full. "Watson" is dozing in an armchair. "Holmes" taps him sharply with his bow

"Watson" What's that? Ah, Holmes! Time for tea, is it?

"Holmes" Really, Watson, I find this love affair with your digestive tract infinitely depressing.

"Watson" Sorry, Holmes. I'm just a bit peckish, that's all.

"Holmes" And being a creature of habit you are no doubt anticipating one of Mrs Hudson's considerable teas?

"Watson" Rather!

"Holmes" Then kindly ring the bell and put yourself out of your misery.

"Watson" gets up to ring the bell. "Holmes" starts to play again, excruciatingly

"Holmes" Did you know, Watson, that some people actually believe Paganini to be possessed by the Devil himself?

"Watson" You don't say so?

"Holmes" The reason being that they believe his incredible technical virtuosity cannot be entirely human.

"Watson" Not a problem you're likely to face, Holmes, if you don't mind me saying so.

The door opens and "Mrs Hudson" enters, groaning under the weight of an enormously loaded tray

Ah! Mrs Hudson! Tea!
"Mrs Hudson" Only a light snack I'm afraid, gentlemen. My niece is poorly.
"Watson" No matter. We shall manage, I'm sure.

"Mrs Hudson" curtsies and exits

Oho! I see a plate of Mrs Hudson's home-made scones!
"Holmes" Then tuck in, my dear fellow! Though personally I find such fare plays havoc with my canal.
"Watson" Canal, Holmes?
"Holmes" Alimentary. My dear Watson, for a man of medicine I find your knowledge of anatomy singularly lacking. I shall aid your digestion with a selection from the Red-Headed Priest! Not to be confused with *The Red-Headed League! (He laughs at his own joke and launches into an appalling version of "The Four Seasons")*
"Watson" (*uncertainly*) Er, most considerate, Holmes.

"Holmes" continues playing and "Watson" starts to eat

The door flies open and Sylvia rushes in. The audience should be made aware of the incongruity of her being in clothes that owe nothing to the Victorian era

Sylvia Rodney, Rodney!

"Holmes" stops playing

Rodney (*dropping the "Holmes" manner*) How many times must I tell you not to burst in like this Sylvia? George and I had just got to a crucial stage!

"Mrs Hudson"/Edna enters

Edna I tried to tell her, Mr Carson, but she wouldn't have none of it, nor would she.
Rodney All right, Edna. It's not your fault. I know how very difficult my wife can be at times.
Sylvia Charming man.
Rodney Sylvia, Sylvia, I can't seem to impress upon you the importance of what we're doing here can I? George and

myself—and Edna, of course—are engaged in a project of the utmost magnitude. By the way, Edna, you can wait outside now. My wife and I are going to have a row.

Edna Thank you very much, sir, I'll do that. God bless you.

Edna exits

Sylvia Fancy making her go through all this. Poor old soul.

Rodney Poor old soul! Poor old soul! She loves it! Didn't you catch that look of pathetic servitude on her face? Give Edna the chance to grovel to her betters and she'll seize it with both knees; and what better way to do that than to play Mrs Hudson to the Great Detective? Edna's a real find, Edna is. I pride myself that it was I who found her on her knees washing the floors at the office.

Sylvia Children, that's all you are! Big kids dressing up.

Rodney You know better than that, Sylvia. It's not every day that one gets the chance to provide the dramatic interlude at the Annual Congress of the Sherlock Holmes Society. George and I are deeply aware of the honour being paid us, aren't we, George?

George Rather.

Rodney And as the big day is tomorrow we need to practise, so if you don't mind . . . ?

Sylvia Every Friday night for the last ten years you've locked yourselves away in here. Is it too much to ask just to see you now and then?

Rodney It's important to me.

Sylvia It's an obsession.

Rodney Nonsense.

Sylvia Some husbands lose themselves in the garden. Some wives are golf-widows. Other men keep exotic and beautiful tropical fish. I had to marry Sherlock Holmes.

Rodney That's right, my darling, off you go . . .

Sylvia But the 'phone call!

Rodney What 'phone call?

Sylvia The police: they've been round to the office.

Rodney The police!

Sylvia Yes, Rodney, the police! Not the Gas Board, not someone collecting for Oxfam, but the police have visited your office!

George Sounds serious.

Sylvia They want to see you. There's an Inspector on his way round.

George Do you think somebody's broken in?

Rodney To a company making security alarms? Did they say what it was about?

Sylvia Said they couldn't divulge that on the 'phone.

George Sounds serious.

Rodney Will you stop saying that, George? You sound like a mynah bird with a severely limited vocabulary. Thank you, Sylvia. I perceive that there is nothing to be done until the Inspector calls. Just time for a quick snatch of *The Six Napoleons* I think, George?

Sylvia Kids!

Rodney Thank you, Sylvia. That will do.

Sylvia exits

Rodney I perceive that the female menopause is wreaking its accustomed havoc.

George I say, Rodney! A real policeman!

Rodney Oh not you too, George? I expected better from you.

George But a real live detective! We might pick up some tips.

Rodney From the official force? (*He snorts contemptuously*)

George No but, really . . . Rodney . . .

Rodney George, George—whilst I appreciate that life may not exactly be all *go* in the heady world of quantity surveying, I little thought that you, of all people, would fall prey to the mistake of expecting any *real* achievement from the regulars. They have no art, no finesse in the matter of detection. Have you learned nothing from the Great Detective? Read your Holmes, George, it's all there. And now, *The Six Napoleons.*

George Rodney?

Rodney What is it now, George?

George Can I ask you something?

Rodney You undoubtedly *can*, George, yes.

George Couldn't I play Holmes? Just this once?

Rodney We've been through all this before.

George It's not much to ask, is it?

Rodney Ask yourself—have you the stature, George? The hawk-like nose? The aquiline features? Have you, would you say, the incisive logic, the shrewd perception, the sheer strength of will to play the Great Man? Of course you haven't. It's absurd.

George You never let me play Holmes.

Rodney George, Nature, in all her infinite wisdom has not cut you out to be a Holmes. You are, and always will be, one of life's Watsons. As Horatio was to Hamlet, as Sancho Panza to Don Quixote, as Tonto to the Lone Ranger—so you are, George, to me. And now, Watson, as I recall the case began with yet another storm-lashed Victorian evening in old Baker Street . . . (*He settles himself in a chair in Holmes-like posture*)

George sighs deeply; he has done it all before

George It was in the early Spring of 1898 that Holmes, having finished with the long and drawn out matter of *The Second Stain*, sat in our rooms in Baker Street. I could tell that he had sunk into one of the most melancholy of his frequent depressions . . .

Rodney I despair of the mentality of the modern criminal, Watson. There are no longer any cases worthy of my abilities. I honestly believe that the age of the extraordinary crime is at an end . . .

George With these words he gave a sigh that wracked his whole being. I saw with considerable trepidation, that before long he would be resorting to the hellish comforts of cocaine in a seven per cent solution. At that moment, however, a short, ferret-like man entered our apartments—

Inspector Jobling, a short, ferret-like man, enters

—bringing Holmes out of his extraordinary lethargy . . .

Rodney leaps to his feet to greet Jobling

Inspector Lestrade of Scotland Yard. One of the foremost detectives of the official force.

Rodney My dear Inspector!

Jobling (*taken aback*) Good evening, sir. I've come . . .

Rodney Not another word, man! Not another word! A brandy and soda for the good Inspector, Watson!

George goes towards the drinks table

Jobling Not while I'm on duty, sir.

Rodney The stock response of the regular force! Good old Lestrade! Now then, I perceive that you walked part of the way here from the Yard and then took a four-wheeler . . .

Jobling No sir, actually I . . .

Rodney And that you have recently been down in East Sussex—
I see the red loam on your boots—where you met with a man
of unsound constitution, a Freemason who suffered sporadic
attacks of asthma.

Jobling This is all very interesting, sir, but . . .

Rodney Nothing, Lestrade, I do assure you. Nothing but observation and the application of logic. And now, the matter upon
which you have come to consult me?

Jobling If I could just get a few things straight, sir?

Rodney No, no! You must leave that to *me*, Inspector!

Jobling And you would be?

Rodney Oh come, come, we know each other well enough, I
think? But I perceive that you must be humoured. My name is
Holmes. Sherlock Holmes.

Jobling starts to write it down and then realization dawns

Jobling Most amusing, sir. And I suppose this would be Doctor
Watson, would it?

Rodney But naturally!

George Rodney—I think this is going a little far, isn't it?

Rodney There's nasty work afoot, I'll be bound?

Jobling Very nasty, sir. And just for the record, ny name's
Jobling. Inspector Jobling. Fraud Squad.

Rodney My apologies, Inspector. George and I have a little
hobby. We get carried away sometimes.

Jobling What you get up to in the privacy of your own home is
your affair, sir. Your real name?

Rodney Carson. Rodney Carson.

Jobling And you are the Managing Director of the Argus
Security Alarm Company?

Rodney I am.

Jobling And this is?

George George Humby. F.R.S.Q.S.

Jobling Now we're getting somewhere. I told your wife, sir, that
due to information from a certain source we had cause to visit
the offices of your company to examine some of the financial
records there.

Rodney Did you have a . . . ?

Jobling takes a warrant from his pocket and waves it in the air

Ah.

Jobling On the basis of a very brief examination it appears that there are certain discrepancies. Financial discrepancies.

Rodney How much?

Jobling We've only formed a very rough idea, you understand. But we estimate that the amount missing runs at about three hundred.

Rodney Three hundred? (*He laughs contemptuously*)

Jobling Thousand, sir.

Rodney is astounded. George gets a brandy and soda and gives it to Rodney, who downs it in one gulp and collapses into a chair

I assume that you're insured for that amount, sir?

Rodney Yes, yes, of course. Charles would have . . . (*He stops as he slowly realizes*)

Jobling Would that be a Mr Charles Meaning?

Rodney Yes.

Jobling The Financial Director of your company?

Rodney nods

Yes. We're very eager to trace Mr Meaning. He seems to have disappeared.

George What, old Charles?

Jobling Of course, there might well be a perfectly simple explanation, but if there is his wife doesn't know about it.

George He's gone? Without Moira?

Jobling Normally we wouldn't worry, but because of the sum involved . . .

Rodney Of course, of course . . .

The Policeman's Chorus from "The Pirates of Penzance" is heard faintly offstage. Throughout the following it becomes gradually louder

George You think that Charles has been cooking the books?

Jobling It seems a possibility, yes, sir.

Rodney Impossible! I'd have trusted Charles with my life. The Board and I were more than happy to leave all the money in Charles's hands.

Jobling And that's just where it seems to have stayed, sir. I've seen it all before. A man in that responsible position—well, he might handle things in an impeccably professional manner for years and then, for reason or reasons unknown, it occurs to him to start fiddling. Every man has his price in my experience.

Rodney A sad reflection on human nature, Inspector.

Jobling It is, sir. Is there anything else you'd like to tell me?

Rodney Not that I can think of.

Jobling When was the last time you saw Mr Meaning, sir?

Rodney Earlier this evening as a matter of fact. He came round for a drink after work.

Jobling And that would have been?

Rodney Oh, about six.

Jobling I might still get the airports sealed in time. He seemed all right, did he?

Rodney He was—well—a little on edge?

Jobling Not surprising really.

Rodney What I can't understand is that *if* he'd embezzled all that money why, in God's name, would he come round for a drink with his Managing Director a few moments before fleeing?

Jobling Hard to say, sir. Men in that position don't behave logically in my experience. To gloat, perhaps? To put up a metaphorical two fingers at the man he'd cheated? Who knows. Well, I'd better be off.

By now the offstage singing has reached a crescendo

Rodney Inspector. There is one question I'd like to ask.

Jobling Ask away, sir.

Rodney What the hell is that unholy row?

Jobling (*offended*) That, sir, is the Chorus of The Metropolitan Opera Company.

Rodney Of New York?

Jobling No, sir. "C" Division. I was called away from a rehearsal to go to your office and I thought I might need some assistance. The lads are getting some practice out in the van. We're doing *The Pirates of Penzance* this year. Rather good, even if I do say so myself. I don't suppose that I could interest you in a few tickets, could I?

Rodney Well, in the circumstances . . .

Jobling Quite so, sir. Not the moment, I see that. We don't seem to have sold many tickets as yet.

Rodney You surprise me.

Jobling I'll be off then. I may want to see you again, sir. Would tomorrow be convenient?
Rodney Of course.
Jobling Good night, then, sir. Doctor.

Jobling goes out but returns instantly

Did you hear that? I called him doctor! (*He laughs*) I'll be pulling in Professor Moriarty next, if I'm not careful! Good-night all.

Jobling goes out

George Decent sort of chap.
Rodney For a regular. I never cease to be amazed at the stupidity of the official force.

The offstage singing stops

George Well, who'd have thought it? Old Charles!
Rodney Still waters, George, still waters.
George You're right. Another brandy?
Rodney (*handing George his glass*) Thank you. Still, a useful encounter in terms of new material I suppose.
George (*finding the brandy bottle empty*) Dead. I'll get another bottle, shall I?
Rodney Do.

Rodney does not notice as George goes to the cupboard

If we apply the theories of the Great Detective to this case, George, I see no reason why—(*turning towards George*)—not that cupboard!

At the same instant George opens the cupboard door. Inside, standing stiff and straight, is a man of about fifty. His expression is one of horror and surprise. His general appearance looks very nineteenth-century with a wing-collar, white waistcoat, a frock coat and make-up. A large bloodstain soaks the front of his shirt. George stares at the body in horror, then slams the door shut and leans against it. Rodney turns away

George Rodney, there's a body in this cupboard!
Rodney Observant as ever.

George looks in the cupboard again and then slams the door

George It's Charles! (*He opens the cupboard door and looks again*) He's wearing make-up! (*He looks in then slams the door*) He looks like—like . . .

Rodney Professor Moriarty.

George (*looking again*) Yes.

Rodney That is precisely what he is meant to look like.

George I see. (*After a pause*) Why?

Rodney He had to die.

George You *knew* he was there?

Rodney You don't think he crept in there and quietly passed away of his own accord *without* my knowledge, do you?

George You killed him?

Rodney Does it look like natural causes?

George Why didn't you tell the Inspector?

Rodney I thought he might take it rather badly.

George I don't believe it!

Rodney The evidence is irrefutable.

George You're mad!

Rodney On the contrary, I am brilliantly sane.

George But why did you kill him?

Rodney I can always trust you to arrive at the first question last, can't I?

George But why kill Charles? There's no logic in it!

Rodney On the contrary, my dear Watson, there is a sustained and quite infallible thread of logic running through the whole affair. Piece together what you know, bring your pitifully under-developed sense of order to bear on the matter and there you have all the answers.

George thinks for a moment

George No. No go, I'm afraid.

Rodney The eternal Watson. Allow me to guide you on your tortuous way. You discover the body of Charles Meaning in my cupboard. He is undeniably dead, of a gunshot wound. Quite obviously he had called round to see me.

George After work for a drink. You told the Inspector.

Rodney Good. Now, knowing what you do of Charles—and this alone would have alerted the suspicions of a natural detective— that he was possibly the most unsociable of men and a teetotaller to boot, does it not seem odd that he should break the habits of a lifetime on this one occasion? So why else might he have called on me?

George thinks

George He wanted to tell you something?
Rodney Splendid! Now what might that something be?

George thinks

George That he was embezzling money from the company! And —you lost your temper and shot him!
Rodney Hopelessly illogical! I could have told the police and had him arrested. Much less messy. So why kill him?

George thinks

George No good.
Rodney For a brief moment, George, I held high hopes for you. Charles told me that I was embezzling money from the company.
George You didn't know?
Rodney Of course I knew! Charles had done an audit and found me out, then came round to tell me that he'd found me out. His big mistake, of course. I had no alternative but to kill him. Logical, isn't it?
George But...
Rodney Yes?
George It's your company.
Rodney Yes.
George So why embezzle money from yourself?
Rodney Logically, who better to embezzle it from?
George I see. No I don't. You're robbing yourself!
Rodney And the taxman, George. And the taxman.
George Ah.
Rodney The trouble with this country today, George, is that all initiative is stifled by the prohibitive tax system. Men of vision and enterprise—like myself—find little incentive to make a profit because of it. That, plus the fact that I am growing a little weary of Sylvia's continuous moans and groans, induced me to this somewhat draconian course of action.
George Where's the money?
Rodney Switzerland. I planned to retire very soon. I've invested

in a shamelessly luxurious chalet overlooking the Reichenbach
Falls.

George Nice.

Rodney There I intended to live out the rest of my days research-
ing into the literary precedents of Holmes and Moriarty.

George Ah, now that's another thing. Why—?

Rodney —is Charles dressed as Moriarty? A good point, Watson,
but quite elementary. Apart from the fact that it provided a
certain dramatic symmetry—what aspiring Sherlock Holmes
would not jump at the chance of killing a Moriarty?

George Sick.

Rodney Perhaps. But expedient too. It's a very hard thing to kill
a man in cold blood, George, especially an amiable dimwit
like Charles. I needed to feel anger, resentment, fury to do it.
You know how the epic struggle at Reichenbach never fails to
disturb my equanamity: we struggled, my anger mounted, I
drew the pistol and shot him. Obviously I needed to drown the
noise of the shot—what better than the music of Wagner and
the deafening thunder of the Falls?

*Rodney turns on the tape recorder and "The Ride of the Valkyries"
and sound of rushing water is heard as at the opening. He lets it
play for a moment and then turns it off*

George But how on earth did you—?

Rodney —persuade him to dress up as Moriarty? Simplicity
itself. I merely told him that we needed a Moriarty for our
little show tomorrow and Charles agreed to do it with alacrity.
He was really very good as well—something I'd not suspected
in him. Quite an actor at heart. He never got as far as accusing
me of fraud, but I knew that he knew, so I killed him. Logical,
is it not? As most things are.

George Morbid, more like. (*He moves to the door*)

Rodney Where are you going?

George To fetch the police, of course.

Rodney (*drawing out the pistol*) I think not, Watson.

George Now hold on—you told me you couldn't kill in cold
blood.

Rodney Not a problem I'll face a second time. Murder hardens
the will. Say good-bye, George, you're going for a swim.

Rodney turns on the tape recorder and aims the pistol at George

As he is about to fire Sylvia bursts in and Rodney quickly hides the pistol

Sylvia Will you turn that row off?

Rodney turns off the tape recoder

George Sylvia, thank God! Listen . . .

Sylvia Not now, George dear. Rodney, Moira Meaning is here. She's in a dreadful state and . . .

Moira enters obviously upset and worried. She is a still attractive woman in her forties

Moira Oh Rodney! Is Charles here?

George As a matter of fact . . .

Rodney Why should Charles be *here*, Moira?

Moira I don't know. The police have been round. Apparently he's done something awful and . . . I can't hold it in any longer! I've killed him! I've killed Charles!

There is general amazement. Pause

Rodney What did you say, Moira?

Moira I've killed Charles!

Sylvia When?

Moira This morning.

Sylvia So why are you looking for him?

Moira It suddenly occurred to me. He's wandering around somewhere. He could drop down at any moment, anywhere. And I thought—well, he might not have changed his underwear this morning. I couldn't stand the shame if he hadn't!

Sylvia But if you've killed him . . . ?

Rodney Precisely. The whole thing's impossible. For more reasons than you know.

George He's right. In fact . . .

Moira This morning I put poison in his tea. A slow-acting poison. It must have worked by now! It must!

Rodney But this is nonsensical! It can't be so! I won't let it be so. *I* killed Charles! You can't take that away from me! I have committed the perfect, logically justifiable crime! And now, for God knows what ragbag of unfounded reasons you've thwarted me! I don't believe it. Logic always triumphs!

Sylvia You killed him?

Rodney Show her, George.

George opens the cupboard

   See? Gunshot wound between the third and fourth rib.
Moira What time did you shoot him?
Rodney About six.
Moira When the poison must have worked.
Rodney Then I might not have been the murderer? I can't
   handle it.
George Aren't any of you going to say "poor old Charles" or
   something similar?
Moira Let me look. (*She goes to the cupboard and examines his
   underwear. She leaves the door open*) Well, that's a weight off
   my mind anyway.
Rodney Since his underwear is covered in blood, I hardly see . . .
George Why did you kill him?
Moira He was being unfaithful.
George What—old Charles?

George and Rodney find this enormously funny

Sylvia What's so funny?
Rodney Well—the idea of old Charles . . .
George He used to get blood pressure at the lingerie adverts on
   the tube.
Sylvia Why do you always say "old Charles"? He was only
   fifty-two.
Rodney Well, he was old before his time, wasn't he?
George Regular old woman.
Rodney And the thought of him with a mistress! Well . . .

Rodney and George giggle

Sylvia As a matter of fact Charles was a marvellous lover.
Rodney Oh come on, Sylvia, you can't . . . (*He begins to realize*)
   How do you know?
Sylvia Simply marvellous.
Moira Sylvia . . .
Sylvia Kind, considerate, selfless—everything that you're not,
   Rodney.
Rodney You're not trying to tell me that—*you*!
Sylvia We were very much in love.

Moira I don't believe it!

Sylvia I've never been happier with anybody. Never. He made me feel like a woman again. After all the years of neglect with you, Rodney, I was fulfilled! Complete! Whole! And I killed him! (*She starts to cry*)

Rodney This is all very well, Sylvia, but you can't just go around having affairs all over the place when it suits you. It's not orderly.

Moira It's you I should have poisoned!

George Hold on, hold on. I might be going deaf or something, but did you say that *you'd* killed him?

Sylvia nods

Rodney Oh no.

Moira You can't have done!

Sylvia I can. Oh God, I can't stand it! The one man I've ever loved!

Rodney I've heard enough of this illogical nonsense!

Sylvia We had it planned. Tonight, when he arrived, I was to put a lethal poison in the drinks. I did. Charles took the wrong one. Poor Charles. He never was much good at conspiracies. He hadn't the nerve for it.

Rodney I remember! I got his lemonade instead of my gin and tonic. I remarked upon it—hold on, hold on! Think, Rodney, think! Hold on to it—Charles got the *wrong* drink and . . . you were trying to kill *me*!

Sylvia And it all went wrong! Horribly, horribly wrong!

George What a tragic misfortune.

Rodney Thank you very much, George. (*To Sylvia*) You were trying to kill me!

Sylvia Well, you don't think I was trying to kill Charles, do you? The only man I've ever loved, the only man who . . .

Rodney All right, all right! Don't start that again, for God's sake! But why? Why kill me?

Sylvia You can ask me that?

Rodney Obviously I *can*. I just did!

Sylvia You're selfish, vain, mean, self-obsessed, intolerant and cruel.

Rodney Yes, all right, but why did you want to kill me?

Sylvia I didn't want to kill you. I wanted to kill bloody Sherlock Holmes!

Rodney Now that's going too far, Sylvia.

Sylvia You didn't have to live with it for year after year. All those silly voices, all those absurd costumes. "I perceive this" and "I deduce that"—you can't *live* with logic, Rodney! I was going mad. Charles saved me and I saw what I had to do.

Rodney You can be very hurtful at times, Sylvia. A man's got to have his hobbies.

Sylvia Hobbies are one thing. Obsessions are another.

George Look, this is all very well, but there's a dead man in the cupboard.

Rodney And I killed him!

Moira No you didn't!

Sylvia Well, if it comes to that you certainly didn't—

George Will you all be quiet? Good. Now then, let's sit down and talk about this rationally.

Rodney An admirable idea, Watson.

Sylvia See what I mean?

Rodney What is needed is the keen insight and incisive mind of a remarkable man to set the whole thing into perspective. Allow me. Now, early this morning Moira, in a fit of envy, doses Charles with a poison that she hopes will kill him later in the day. At six this evening, Charles, on my invitation, arrives at what he thinks is going to be a social occasion . . .

Moira Then why is he dressed as . . .?

George Better not to ask, Moira, believe me.

Rodney My darling wife, Sylvia, intent on murdering me, does not count on Charles's usual blithering incompetence and, rather than poisoning me as planned—I'll speak to you later, Sylvia —sees with horror that her lover . . . I say, George, old Charles!

George and Rodney giggle

Sylvia Rodney!

Rodney Sorry. Sees Charles down the fatal brew. A few moments later, in rather bizarre circumstances, I shoot Charles and hide him in the cupboard as I hear George arriving for our rehearsal. Well now, that seems to me to be a perfectly acceptable résumé of the events. Logic has, as usual, triumphed over disorder and chaos.

George But in that case which of you three *did* kill the poor
   fellow?

Rodney Logically speaking all of us. Or none of us. It depends
   which way you look at it. Well, I find that very satisfactory.
   Very satisfactory indeed.

The doorbell rings

   And logically that should be the police come hot-foot from the
   nick, too late as usual.

Sylvia I'll go. Er . . . (*She points at the cupboard*)

George Ah yes. (*He shuts the door*) I hope you'll remember that
   I had nothing to do with this?

   Sylvia goes out

Rodney George, not even a man as stupid as the Inspector could
   ever think that you had the brains or initiative for such an act.

George Thank you.

   *Sylvia enters with Glenda, Charles's secretary. She is in her
   twenties, an attractive, rather intimidating young woman*

Sylvia It's, er—

Glenda Glenda.

Rodney Of course.

Glenda Charles's secretary and personal assistant.

Rodney Quite so.

Glenda *Very* personal sometimes.

Rodney Yes, I don't think you've met Charles's *wife*, have you,
   Glenda? Moira, Glenda, Glenda, Moira.

Glenda and Moira nod frostily

   Oh, and George. George, Glenda, Glenda, George.

Sylvia That'll do, Rodney.

Rodney Sylvia, my wife. Sylvia, Glenda, Glenda—

Sylvia Shut up, Rodney.

Rodney Yes.

There is silence

Rodney Well, I expect we're all wondering what you're doing
   here, Glenda? What with it being after hours and everything.

Rodney looks around but there is no response

Well, I'm certainly wondering and I expect all the others are wondering too, except that they . . .

Sylvia Rodney.

Glenda It's no secret. I'm looking for Charles.

Rodney
George
Sylvia } *(together)* { *Why?*
Moira

Glenda I could say that I've got some letters for him to sign.

Moira And have you?

Glenda No. The truth is that I arranged to meet him after work and he didn't show up. I knew—he told me—that he was coming around here for a rehearsal.

Moira Rehearsal?

George puts his fingers to his lips and shakes his head. Moira shrugs

Glenda So naturally this is the first place that I came.

Moira And?

Glenda I beg your pardon?

Sylvia And?

Glenda (*looking round them all*) Oh dear, I've compromised myself, haven't I?

George *Have* you?

Glenda I've no choice but to tell you. It might be better this way. The fact is that Charles and I were to run away together tonight.

Moira *What?*

Glenda I'm sorry Mrs Meaning, but that's the way it is.

George Was.

Glenda Charles and I are lovers.

George Were.

Glenda I'm sorry, but do you know something that I don't?

George I rather think that we do, yes.

Glenda What?

George Well, I'd try to get a quick refund on the air tickets if I were you.

George opens the cupboard door. Glenda gives a short scream

Glenda Oh God!

George Quite so.

Rodney Quite a dark horse, Old Charles, eh George?

George and Rodney start to giggle again

Sylvia I fail to see what's funny.

Rodney Oh come on! Old Charles spends years as the respectable accountant plodding away full of *Sanatogen* and *Yeast-Vite*, then all of a sudden—wham, bang—

Moira You might have phrased it better.

Rodney —there he is having an affair with you *and* Glenda here! No wonder he aged prematurely.

George and Rodney laugh

Glenda He always said that ours was a heaven made match.

Rodney Perhaps he's just gone to check on the contract.

Glenda He said that after he'd got enough from embezzling the company we'd go away together. And then he goes and dies!

George Not exactly his fault. Circumstances beyond his control.

Rodney Wait a minute, wait a minute! Did you say that *Charles* was embezzling the company?

Glenda Three hundred thousand at the last count.

Rodney No, no, I was embezzling the company! Me! Rodney!

Glenda That was the funny part. You thought you were, but old Charles was at least three jumps ahead of you. You're not a qualified accountant, he was. He let you *think* you were being terribly clever but all the money was going to his account in the Seychelles. You've been tricked, Mr Carson.

Rodney That seems logical. No, what am I saying? It's absurd!

Glenda It's the truth.

Rodney Hold on. Think, Rodney, piece it together. If Charles was defrauding the firm then logically there was no need for me to kill him!

Glenda *You* killed him?

Rodney I have a tentative claim, yes. The exact details aren't clear as yet. Glenda—*you* didn't try to kill him, did you?

Glenda Me? No! Why should I?

Rodney Thank God for that. A grain of logic anyway. At least this has cleared the air and we all know where we stand. If there is one thing that I cannot stomach it is confusion.

There is a terrible wailing off stage

Oh Christ.

Edna enters at a pace then falls to her knees, her hands clasped in fervent prayer

Edna Holy Mary, Mother of God, forgive me, for I have sinned!
Rodney You have *feet*, Edna! In God's name, use them!
Edna Thank you, sir. But I feel happier on my knees.
Rodney What did I tell you, Sylvia?
Edna Oh, how I have sinned. I can hold it in no longer or my soul will burst! I must confess in the sight of the Almighty Himself!
Rodney We can't quite run to that, Edna. Would we do instead? Although I've a nasty feeling what it is you're going to tell us.
Edna I have killed a man today!
Rodney Well, life *is* full of little surprises, isn't it? And who would this be, Edna? As if we didn't know.
Edna It is none other than Mr Meaning himself!
Rodney Do you remember my remarking, Watson, that I despaired of the criminal mind? Perhaps you'd care to tell us how you achieved this remarkable feat?
Edna Tonight, before the man himself left the office...
Sylvia That's Mr Meaning?
Edna Rest his soul. Before he left I slipped him some ground glass in his tea. Oh, Holy Father forgive me!
Rodney If he does it'll be on overtime. If Charles doesn't look out he's going to end up as a walking compendium of fiendish crime.
Sylvia Hardly walking.
Edna When I think of what that glass must have done to his poor stomach, his kidneys, his...
George Thank you, Edna, that'll do.
Rodney I suppose one must ask the inevitable question. Why, Edna, why?
Edna I couldn't stand it any longer, sir. The way he used to treat me at work. Until a couple of months ago he was sweetness itself, a real gentleman, he was. Then he started acting peculiar: kicking me up the bum—God forgive me—when I was on my knees washing the floors, treading on my knuckles and laughing like Old Nick himself and all sorts of other things that I can't bring myself to mention. And him such a gent before. To say nothing of Deirdre.

George Deirdre?

Edna My little girl. Well, not so little now, as a matter of fact. Oh, I don't know as I can say it in front of poor Mrs Meaning here . . .

Moira It doesn't seem to have stopped anyone else, so you might as well.

Edna I swear by all the angels that I didn't know nothing about it until it was too late. Mr Meaning started seeing Deidre and . . . well, the long and the short of it, sir, is that she is with child by him!

Rodney I don't believe it!

Rodney and George start to laugh

Edna (*shouting loudly*) Deirdre, will you get yourself in here now?

The door opens and a girl, hugely pregnant, staggers in

There now, will you only use your eyes?

Rodney *Quod est demonstrandum.*

Edna Now, Deirdre, will you tell the good people here who it was who got you into this unholy state?

Deidre Sure, and I don't like to, Mam.

Edna You tell them, Deirdre O'Fergus, or you'll feel the back of my hand, babe or no babe, that you will!

George Perhaps I can be of assistance. Do you recognize *this* man? (*He opens the cupboard door*)

Deirdre screams and faints

George Enough said.

Edna Ah well, he looks at peace now, rest his soul.

Charles's expression hardly justifies this. Rodney and George do a double-take and shrug

Rodney This has all got rather beyond me.

Deirdre starts to moan. Her cries become more and more fervent

Edna Holy Mother! She's starting!

Rodney Starting what?

Sylvia For heaven's sake, Rodney! She's going into labour!

Rodney What! In my house?

Moira Well don't just stand there! Do something!

Rodney You heard them, George! Do something!
George Why me?
Rodney You're the doctor, aren't you?
George Oh yes. (*He moves towards Deirdre and then stops*) No,
   I'm not, I'm a quantity surveyor!
Rodney Excuses, that's all I get from you.
George Um, er, ah! Hot water and plenty of it!
Rodney What are you going to do? Boil the brat?
George I don't know! They always say that!
Edna Oh my poor little girl!

*Faint singing of the Policeman's Chorus can be heard offstage as
before, increasing in volume*

   Inspector Jobling enters

Jobling Don't anybody move! I've got the house surrounded!
Rodney So we hear. You're a policeman. Do something!
Jobling (*surveying the scene*) Sorry. We don't get a lot of call for
   this sort of thing in the Fraud Squad. It's all paperwork, see?
Rodney I sometimes wonder what I pay my rates for.
Edna If it's a boy we'll call it Charles.
Moira That's very sweet of you.
Edna Sure and it's the least we can do, after all the trouble we've
   caused you.
Rodney Inspector, what are you doing back here?
Jobling In point of fact, sir, I've never been away. Unbeknownst
   to you I left a small microphone behind when I left. I've been
   out in the van recording every single word that has been said
   in this room. As Mr Holmes might say, my evidence is irrefutable!

*With a flourish of triumph he produces a small tape recorder and
presses the button. The Policeman's Chorus from "The Pirates of
Penzance" can be heard. After a short pause he quickly switches off
the recorder*

   Yes, well . . . (*He is highly embarrassed*)
Rodney One thing has been puzzling me, Inspector. How did you
   know about all this to start with? Who *was* the certain source
   you mentioned earlier?
George I'm rather afraid it was me, Rodney.
Rodney You, Watson? You are the snake in the grass?

Jobling That's right, sir. Mr Humby came to us some weeks ago and told us he thought there was something fishy going on. I didn't expect to find Gala night in Grimsby, though.

Rodney Well, George, I hope you feel pleased with yourself?

George Only doing my duty as a public spirited citizen.

Jobling Very commendable, sir. Except for one thing.

George What's that?

Jobling We know a thing or two about logic on the force as well. Who in their right minds grasses on a friend—or friends—and expects nothing in return? Nobody. It therefore follows that when you came to me with your suspicions you had an ulterior motive. Who does anything out of a feeling of public spirit any more? It therefore follows that you have an interest in the case. Logically I deduced that you came to us out of feelings of resentment and envy. Everybody else seemed to be leading such complicated, enjoyable lives and you couldn't bear to be left out, could you, Humby? So logically the thing to do was to make yourself feel important. How do you do that? How do you draw attention to yourself? By killing somebody! By killing Charles Aloysius Meaning!

Rodney Bravo, Inspector! You really have come on apace!

George But it's not true! I didn't kill Charles! I acted out of the best of motives! Totally selflessly!

Rodney And ask yourself, George: is that logical?

George thinks for a moment

George I suppose not. Clap them on, Inspector.

Jobling handcuffs George

Rodney A very satisfactory conclusion to the case, Inspector. Neatly wrapped up.

The cupboard door begins to rattle violently

Oh God no.

The door bursts open and Charles staggers out. There is general horror. Bleeding horribly and in great pain, he goes towards the Inspector. With a trembling, blood-stained hand he pushes a note into the Inspector's hand and then dies, smiling

Rodney Good God!

George But what is it, Inspector?

The Inspector looks up horrified

Jobling It's a suicide note, sir.

Deirdre's moaning and the singing off stage reach a climax

A band of policemen, loosely disguised as the pirates from "The Pirates of Penzance" enter singing "With Cat-Like Tread" (This is optional and may be done as a sound effect offstage)

Rodney holds his head in his hands

BLACK-OUT

CURTAIN

FURNITURE AND PROPERTY LIST

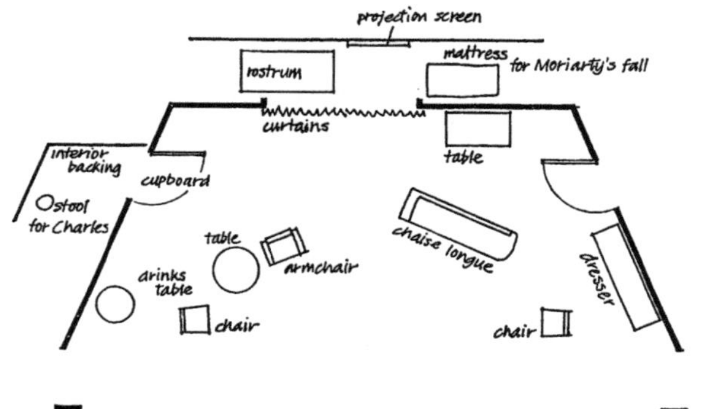

On stage: Armchair
2 upright chairs
Chaise-longue
Table
Drinks table. *On it:* glasses, bottle of brandy, sodasyphon
Table upstage R. *On it:* tape recorder
Dresser. *On it:* chemistry set, books
Projection screen
Mattress (for "**Moriarty's**" fall)
Stool in cupboard (for **Charles**)
Servant's bell

Further dressing may be added to convey the impression of a very untidy cluttered room, with the emphasis on Victoriana

Off stage: Pistol loaded with blanks, violin and bow ("**Holmes**")
Tray loaded with tea-things ("**Mrs Hudson**")
Note-book and pencil, warrant, handcuffs, small portable tape recorder (**Inspector Jobling**)
Suicide note (**Charles**)

LIGHTING PLOT

<table>
<tr><td>Cue 1</td><td>As upstage c curtains open
Silhouette effect on "Holmes" and "Moriarty" struggling
and waterfall effect on projection screen L of
rostrum</td><td>(Page 1)</td></tr>
<tr><td>Cue 2</td><td>As curtains close slowly
Silhouette and waterfall effects fade slowly to
Black-out</td><td>(Page 1)</td></tr>
<tr><td>Cue 3</td><td>After violin playing has stopped
Bring up spot on "Holmes" downstage c</td><td>(Page 2)</td></tr>
<tr><td>Cue 4</td><td>"Holmes": "Watson?"
Bring up lighting to full and fade spot</td><td>(Page 2)</td></tr>
<tr><td>Cue 5</td><td>Rodney holds his head in his hands
Black-out</td><td>(Page 25)</td></tr>
</table>

EFFECTS PLOT

Cue 12   **Rodney** turns on the tape recorder   (Page 13)
           Snap on sound of rushing water and "The Ride of
               the Valkyries" very loudly

Cue 13   **Rodney** turns off the tape recorder   (Page 13)
           Snap off sound of rushing water and "The Ride of
               the Valkyiries"

Cue 14   **Rodney** turns on the tape recorder for the
               second time   (Page 13)
           Repeat cue 12

Cue 15   **Rodney** turns off the tape recorder   (Page 14)
           Repeat cue 13

Cue 16   **Rodney:** "Very satisfactory indeed."   (Page 18)
           Doorbell rings

Cue 17   **Edna:** "Oh my poor little girl!"   (Page 23)
           Faint singing offstage of the Policemen's Chorus as
               before. It increases in volume

Cue 18   **Jobling** switches on small tape recorder   (Page 23)
           Snap on tape of the Policeman's Chorus

Cue 19   **Jobling** quickly switches off small tape recorder   (Page 23)
           Snap off tape of the Policemen's Chorus

Cue* 20   **Jobling: "It's a suicide note, sir."   (Page 25)
           Sound of chorus singing "With Cat-Like Tread"
               offstage, rapidly increasing in volume

* Cues marked with an asterisk are optional effects and may be
performed on stage by the characters concerned

MADE AND PRINTED IN GREAT BRITAIN BY
LATIMER TREND & COMPANY LTD PLYMOUTH
MADE IN ENGLAND

www.ingramcontent.com/pod-product-compliance
Ingram Content Group UK Ltd.
Pitfield, Milton Keynes, MK11 3LW, UK
UKHW021821150726
7214IPUK00017B/244